*I dedicate this book to my sister, Melissa.*

*May your path be blessed and your connections deep.*

# Contents

# Preface

All cultures use mandalas—circular images—to convey the universal concepts that life is a cycle, that all things are one, and that the universe within and the universe without are reflections of each other. Mandalas are powerful universal icons that portray a deep sense of oneness.

I have been immersed in the mandala process for many years, but for a long time there was a part missing for me: a direct connection with Judaism. It was easy to find mandala images in other traditions; I often struggled, however, to find the spiritual connection between mandalas and Judaism.

The connection is not obvious, but it is there. In Kabbalah (the mystical tradition within Judaism), a meditative practice called *sh'viteem* uses Hebrew words, prayers, and/or names of God in special patterns to help focus one's attention toward the center—directing the pray-er toward that place within in which to find connection.

Drawing mandalas for each letter of the Hebrew alphabet seemed to be the appropriate place to begin to incorporate Kabbalistic concepts into my mandala practice. This process began during a one-day silent Kabbalah retreat in the spring of 2001, when I drew the image for aleph. Then, through a connection my mother made, I had an opportunity to exhibit my artwork at the Jewish Community Center of Buffalo, New York. I decided that the show would consist primarily of mandalas for each letter of the aleph-bet.

I began by doing a lot of reading about Kabbalah and the aleph-bet (see "Suggested Reading"). Once I developed a basic understanding of each letter of the aleph-bet, I meditated on the letter and received a symbol that reflected my understanding of the spiritual essence of the letter. After drawing the image of the letter, I meditated with it—in a kind of dialogue with the image—before I began to write the text. Through discussions with rabbis, Kabbalists, and others, I refined the text in numerous iterations.

The images and text reflect my interpretation of each letter. They do not convey everything within the letters, each of which has many layers of meanings. For me, *Songs of Creation* is not the culmination of my learning but the beginning of it.

I hope that *Songs of Creation* will help you connect with the richness of the Jewish mystical tradition, glimpse the infinite possibilities of life and creation, and deepen your spiritual connections. In the process of creating this book, I have learned that we are co-creators with the Divine, that the world is in a constant state of creation, and that we are responsible for the world we create. May we be very conscious and intentional—individually and collectively—in thought, word, and deed and together create a better world.

# Acknowledgments

I believe that when we turn our life over in service of the Divine, miracles happen. This book is one example: Nothing short of Divine inspiration and intervention made it possible. Yet if I had known ahead of time what it would entail, I'm not sure I would have willingly signed up. But I felt the energy within and knew I needed to let it move through. I had to learn to be open to what comes, to neither force it nor restrain it but to let it flow and to keep my ego out of the way. At many points along the way I thought of letting the project go; then the right person would show up at the right time and say just the right thing to keep me on the path. This book has been a team effort. It was created very much in the style of true Torah study, in dialogue and study with others. I want to pay tribute to the many individuals who assisted in the process and helped make this dream a reality.

First and foremost, I thank my mother, Ann Judelsohn, for getting the ball rolling by initiating the conversation that resulted in my show in Buffalo, New York, where I first exhibited the letters of the aleph-bet. She also had a vital part in the initial marketing effort for this book. Without her belief in my dreams and her love, support, and encouragement throughout this process and always, none of this would have happened.

I am grateful to Rev. Sue Greer, who helped me connect more deeply with myself and thereby with the Divine and the world, and who spiritually midwifed many of the images in this book.

Rabbi Jamie Arnold offered very constructive feedback regarding the images and text. My thanks also to Rabbi David Shneyer for his constructive feedback and suggestion to include a kavannah (meditative intention) with each letter.

Thank you to my dear friend Shira Keyes, who devoted endless hours and energy helping me hone the text and provided much advice and assistance as I began to step into my persona and career as an artist.

I thank Jerry Callistein, Judith Cornell, Steve Fox, Rabbi Heschel Greenberg, Ariele Love, Iola Morrisey, Cantor Sunny Schnitzer, and Jesse Stoff for their varied contributions and support. Special thanks to Kathy Strauss and GC Schow, from ImageWerks,lc, for the countless hours and immense energy and creativity they donated to make this book a reality, and for all of their encouragement, friendship, and generosity of spirit.

Finally, all my love and thanks to my husband, David, for sharing my vision and encouraging me to go for it. "Cuz ya know . . . when you make that kind of commitment, you gotta live by it!"

# *Introduction*

*Songs of Creation* is a meditative expression of the Divine energy of the aleph-bet. The text that accompanies each image provides an interpretation of the letter's spiritual meaning and includes a kavannah (meditative intention). You can use the images, the text, or both as focal points for meditation. You can stand this book up on a tabletop or desk to facilitate this meditative practice.

Teachers can use *Songs of Creation* to help students explore the letters of the aleph-bet and to open dialogue on values and ethics. You can use the book as an entry point to exploration of mystical concepts; you may find that it opens doors into your own spiritual journey and sparks contemplation and further study. (At the back of the book I have included a list of suggested readings that have been useful in my journey.) And, of course, you can simply enjoy the artwork for its own sake.

A Kabbalah story tells us that God creates the universe by forming letters and combining them into words. The letters are the building blocks of creation; their potential combinations are infinite. Through the act of speaking, God brings the world into being. The title of this book reflects my belief that perhaps God uses letters, colors, and light to create melodies and harmonies and sings the universe into being: "Uni-verse" literally means "one song." Thus, each image in the book is itself a song.

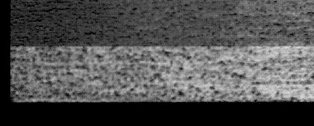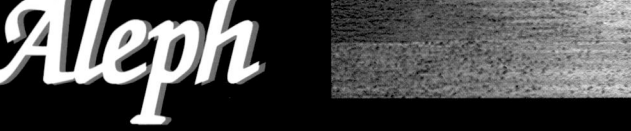

# Aleph

**_Aleph_ is soundless: the sound before sound, the silence between breaths and within breaths.**

_Aleph_ embodies the primordial, Divine potential of the Universe (_olam_). _Aleph_ is formlessness encapsulated in form; it contains everything—and nothing. Prior to the act of creation, God was Boundless Light: unformed and limitless, all potential and possibility. _Aleph_ contains all of the universe's potential and all of its emptiness simultaneously. _Aleph_ represents a dynamic process of movement from unity to diversity and back to unity.

_Kavannah_:
**FOLLOW YOUR BREATH.**
**LISTEN TO THE SOUND OF THE SILENCE.**

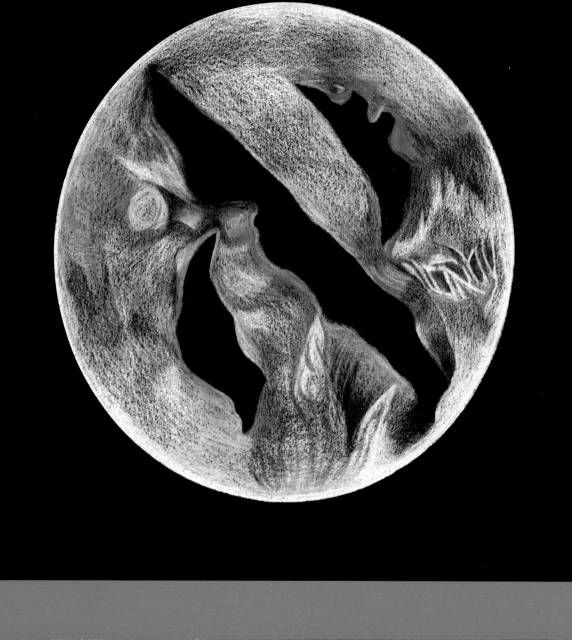

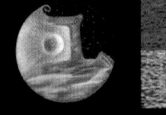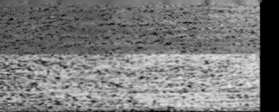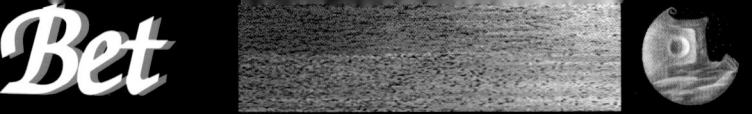

# Bet

**_Bet_ is the sound of God creating the universe through the act of speaking.**

_Bet_ is the second letter of the _aleph-bet_ but the first letter of the Torah: _B'reisheet_ ("With beginningness…"). The creation of the physical world—the place for the Divine Spirit to dwell—began with _bet_. The word _bet_ means house, and the letter is shaped like a structure, with a floor, a wall, a roof, and an opening to enter and exit. The entire world is our home, and the _Shekhina_ (indwelling presence) dwells within us and all things.

_Bet_ represents the illusion of duality: the separation of light from dark, day from night, the seen from the unseen, good from bad, love from fear. By creating these apparent dualities, God creates choice (_b'chirah_).

_Kavannah:_

**REMEMBER THAT IN ALL THINGS YOU HAVE A CHOICE. SEE PAST THE DUALITY TO THE TRUTH: WE ARE ONE; THE WORLD IS ONE; GOD IS ONE.**

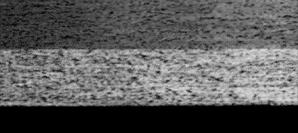

# Gimmel

*Gimmel* **symbolizes the building blocks out of which everything is possible and the eternal life of the soul is sustained.**

The soul continues through eternity, always taking part in the cycle of birth-death-rebirth. The point of light at the center of the image connects the three cycles, which began long before us and will continue endlessly. The three primary colors (red, yellow, and blue) form the background of this image because they are the building blocks of all the other colors.

*Gimmel*, the third letter, also exemplifies the three-way divisions in how we think about our world: thought, word, and action; God, Torah, and Israel; creation, revelation, and redemption; mind, breath, and body.

*Kavannah:*

## HOW DO YOU USE THOUGHTS, WORDS, AND ACTIONS AS BUILDING BLOCKS TO CREATE YOUR LIFE?

## Dalet announces that God is present everywhere, in all things.

God is in the four directions and the four elements—earth, water, fire, and air—that make up the physical world. The tetragrammaton, the unpronounceable name of God, contains four letters: *yod, hey, vav, hey.* And Jewish mysticism (Kabbalah) teaches that there are four worlds: *asiyah* (physical), *yetzirah* (emotional), *b'riyah* (mental), and *atzilut* (spiritual). *Dalet* is the gateway between these four worlds. *Dalet* encourages us to see the truth contained within the physical boundaries of existence.

*Kavannah:*

**TAKE A SELF-INVENTORY OF YOUR PHYSICAL, EMOTIONAL, INTELLECTUAL, AND SPIRITUAL STATE. NOTICE HOW YOU LIVE IN ALL FOUR WORLDS AT THE SAME TIME.**

*Dalet*

# *Hey* is the sound of breath: the breath that permeates the universe, the breath of life.

*Hey* evokes transformation and the power of being. Sarai became Sarah and Avram became Avraham by the insertion of *hey* in their names, thus symbolizing the presence of the breath of God within them and their personal transformations.

In the tetragrammaton, the unpronounceable name of God (*yod-hey-vav-hey*), the first *hey* symbolizes the hand of God reaching toward us; the second *hey* represents our aspiring toward God. *Hey* is how God reaches us and how we reach to God: through breath.

*Kavannah:*

## SIT STILL AND BREATHE. CALM YOUR MIND. BECOME CENTERED. LISTEN FOR THE PRESENCE OF GOD SPEAKING TO YOU.

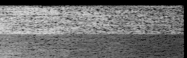

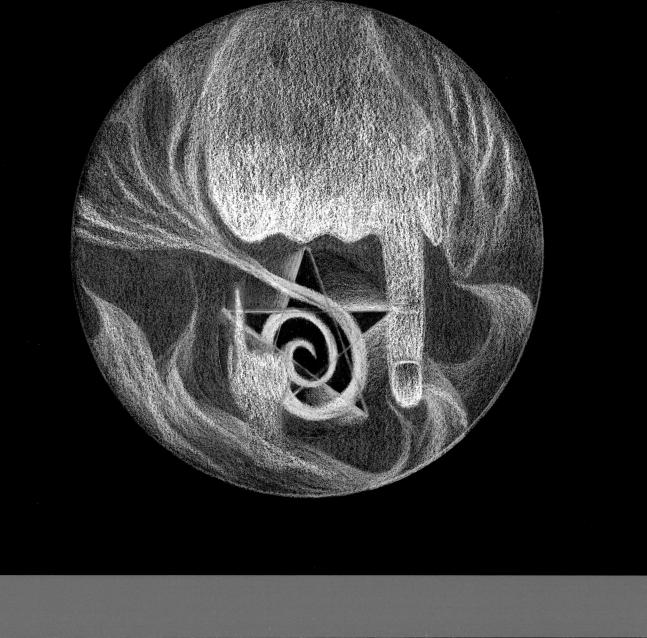

## Vav connects our world and the spiritual world.

Like Jacob's ladder (which connects heaven and earth), *vav* is a link—a Divine mechanism for connecting with God. We connect spiritually with God by performing *mitzvot* (religious obligations). The blessings we offer as we perform these *mitzvot* strengthen our connection with God, as we acknowledge the Divine presence in ourselves, in others, and in the actions we take.

*Vav*, the sixth letter of the *aleph-bet*, links the six directions (east, west, north, south, up, and down); it also represents humanity, which was created on the sixth day, and the Torah, which was revealed on the sixth day of the month of *Sivan*. Yet *vav* resembles the number 1, reminding us that all things are One.

*Kavannah:*

**WE CONNECT WITH THE DIVINE IN MANY WAYS— THROUGH PRAYER, MEDITATION, MITZVOT. HOW DO YOU CLIMB THE LADDER AND CONNECT WITH YOURSELF, OTHERS, AND GOD?**

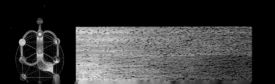

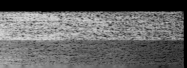

# *Zayin* represents movement and separation.

Shaped like a sword, *zayin* functions as a tool for spiritual discernment and distinction, cutting away what is unholy within us and enabling us to rise to higher levels of spiritual awareness and wisdom.

*Zayin*, the seventh letter of the *aleph-bet*, also represents the Sabbath—the separation of the sacred from the ordinary. After creating the world in the first six days, God took the seventh day to rest. *Zayin* invites us to nourish ourselves physically, emotionally, and spiritually.

*Kavannah:*

**TAKE TIME DAILY TO SEPARATE FROM THE ORDINARY AND CONNECT WITH THE SACRED. TAKE THE SABBATH AND MAKE IT HOLY. TAKE STEPS TO NURTURE YOUR SOUL.**

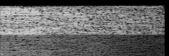

*Zayin*

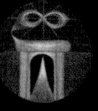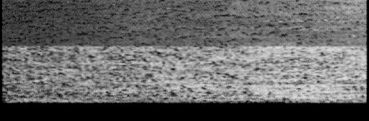 *Chet*

## *Chet* is the gateway into sacred space.

Passing through this gate is like walking into a temple and having faith that God will meet us there, and that life (*chai*) goes on eternally.

Our purpose in life is to meet God daily through acts of lovingkindness (*gemilut chasadim*). When we are acting for a Divine purpose, we are fully alive. *Chet* encourages us to choose life, to rejoice in the infinite source of all creation.

*Kavannah:*
## LIFT UP, GLORIFY, AND SANCTIFY LIFE. COMMIT TO WALKING YOUR PATH.

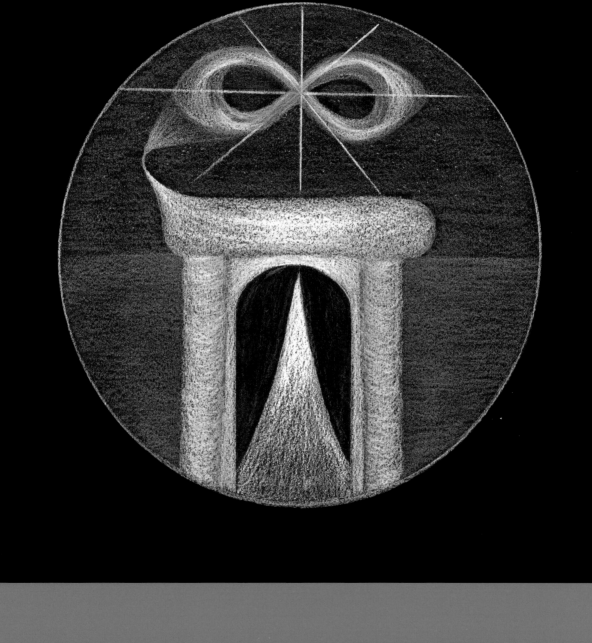

# *Tet* represents goodness in all things.

The goodness (*tov*) in life is glowing all around us, radiant and brilliant. Sometimes goodness is easy to recognize; at other times goodness is hidden. In those difficult times, we are called on to have faith and to search for goodness in the darkness.

From *tet* we learn that a single spark of light is powerful enough to dispel the darkness. *Tet* encourages us to find the light hidden in the dark. It suggests that we look for the God within and the good within.

*Kavannah:*

**BE OBSERVANT. SEE THE GOOD; SEE THE HUMAN SPIRIT RISING TO THE OCCASION, PEOPLE CONNECTING WITH EACH OTHER—SPEAKING KINDLY, EMBRACING, EXPERIENCE HEARTS OPENING.**

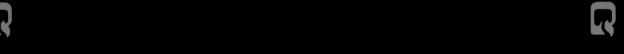

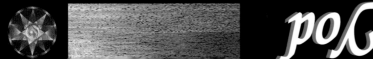

# Yod

**Yod is Divine essence, a precious jewel refracting throughout the universe.**

*Yod*, the tenth letter, embodies all the meanings and essence of the number 10. It reminds us that there are 10 commandments and 10 directions. We have 10 fingers and 10 toes, and we count years in decades. The number 10 also is unitary, which reflects the oneness of monotheism.

*Yod's* tinyness contains so much: All Hebrew letters come from *yod* because each letter begins with the smallest speck—an echo of *yod*, the smallest letter. The tetragrammaton, the unpronounceable name of God, begins with *yod*: *Yod-hey-vav-hey* means that God is all that ever was, is, and will be.

*Yod* suggests that if we gather our diffuse energies and focus them in a single direction, we may become closer to the Divine.

*Kavannah:*

**MANIFEST THE SPIRITUAL IN YOUR DAILY EXISTENCE, CONSCIOUSLY ACTING, CREATING, SPEAKING, AND DOING.**

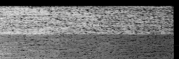

# *Kaf*

*Kaf* contains the dynamic balance between opening
to Divine inspiration and manifesting inspired action.

Just as the ocean is never separate from the shore, God is with us always and
everywhere. As co-creators of our world, we are responsible for giving this Divine essence
conscious form through our thoughts, words, and actions.

When we live with intention (*kavannah*), we walk the path toward God. Through acts of
lovingkindness and righteousness, we raise ourselves up—we open ourselves to Divine
emanations and become receptive to the blessings God may bestow upon us. Through
this cycle of receiving and acting we become vessels for the manifestation of the Divine
in our world.

*Kavannah:*

## HOW DO YOU CONTAIN AND MANIFEST DIVINE
## ESSENCE IN THE WORLD?

# *Lamed*

**Lamed represents study and learning as a path to God.**

*Lamed* is alive, pulsing, moving. Its shape reflects the twists and turns on the path of learning. By following the path upward, we raise ourselves in spiritual connection with the Divine. When we learn through all four worlds—*asiyah* (physical), *yetzirah* (emotional), *b'riyah* (mental), and *atzilut* (spiritual)—we experience integration and our deepest connection to God. Authentic learning requires us to manifest our understanding through our thoughts, words, and actions. Our ultimate goal is transcendence.

*Kavannah:*

**GO FORTH AND LEARN SOMETHING NEW THAT STRENGTHENS YOUR PERSONAL INTEGRATION AND CONNECTION WITH GOD.**

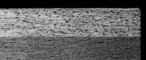

# *Mem* evokes completion and perfection.

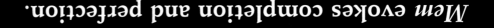

To be complete, we surrender voluntarily to the Divine—bowing down in reverence. In this act of bowing, we are raised up. *Mem* is about having faith in God as the Source of all things. When we surrender to the Divine, all of the abundance of Source is available to us.

*Mem* also reminds us that the world is like a womb; the Waters of Life (*mayim chayim*) nurture and support us, just as the waters of a mother's womb nurture her growing baby. By surrendering to Divine nature within us, we are born into a deeper spiritual connection with life.

*Kavannah:*

**SURRENDER YOURSELF TO THE DIVINE WITHIN.**
**ASK GOD HOW YOU CAN BE OF SERVICE.**

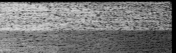

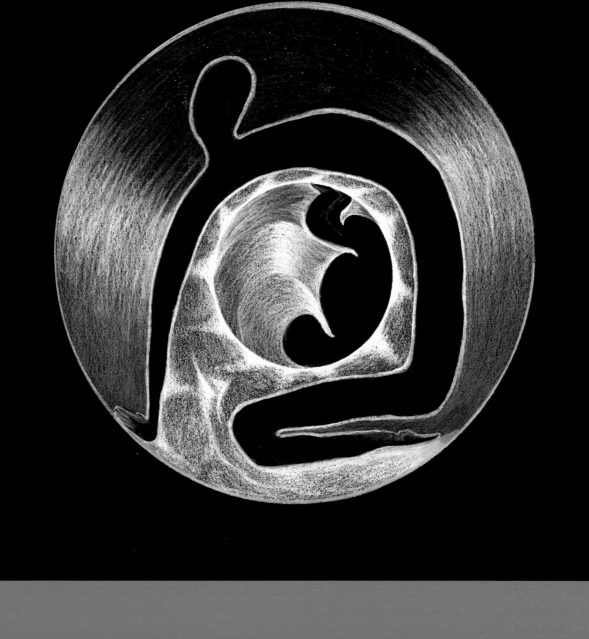

# *Nun* encompasses the process of personal growth.

By growing toward God, we receive God's blessing upon us. Life endures through the cycles of birth, death, and rebirth. We experience times of joy and enlightenment and times of pain and darkness. Like the seed, we grow from darkness to light. This process invites us to have the courage to go down into our own unconscious, seeking the treasure contained within. By bringing the unconscious into the light of day, we create the container to hold the Divine Spirit. *Nun* reminds us that all things are contained within their opposites.

*Kavannah:*

**GENERATE THE COURAGE TO SEE THE LIGHT AND JOY IN TIMES OF DARKNESS. EMBRACE THE IDEA THAT LIFE IS ALWAYS CHANGING. HOW CAN YOU NURTURE THE CHANGES IN YOUR LIFE TOWARD WHOLENESS, LOVE, AND UNITY?**

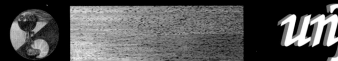

# Samech

**Samech embodies the never-ending cycle of life cradled in the hands of God.**

*Samech* represents the Divine support (*Samech noflim*) that is always available to us. The universe within and the universe without are one. Whether we start at the center and move outward or start on the outside and move inward, we are always Divinely supported. The physical becomes the spiritual becomes the physical: Connecting with the Divine in the spiritual realm results in support in the physical world. By performing acts in service of the Divine and becoming one with God, we create the support structure that facilitates further holiness in our world and the world above.

*Kavannah:*

**CONSIDER HOW YOU SUPPORT OTHERS AND HOW OTHERS SUPPORT YOU. HOW DO YOU GIVE? HOW DO YOU RECEIVE?**

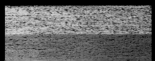

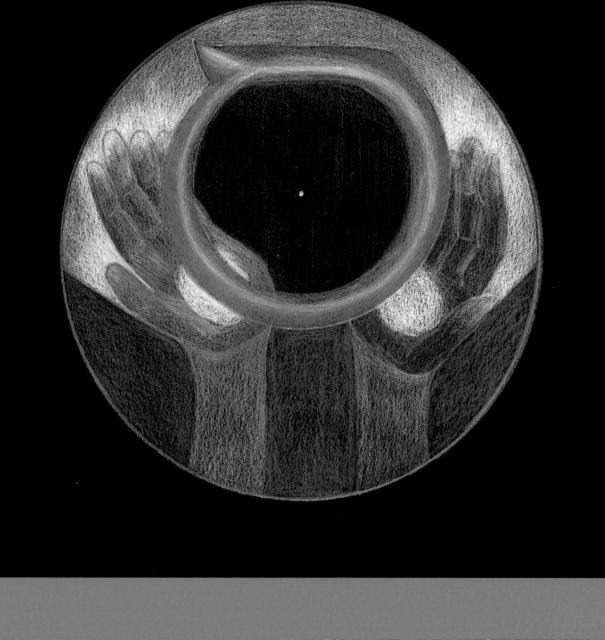

## *Ayin* envisions insight and consciousness.

Opening our eyes, turning our eyes toward God, we see God more clearly and become conscious of something deeper than ordinary physical existence. The hidden aspects of God are revealed to us as we raise our level of consciousness.

Opening our consciousness to God, we understand that life is a path with many choices and options, and everything is a manifestation of the Tree of Life (*Etz Chayim*). The insights we receive expand our hearts.

*Kavannah:*

## CLOSE YOUR EYES AND SEE THE TRUTH WITHIN.

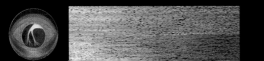

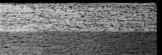

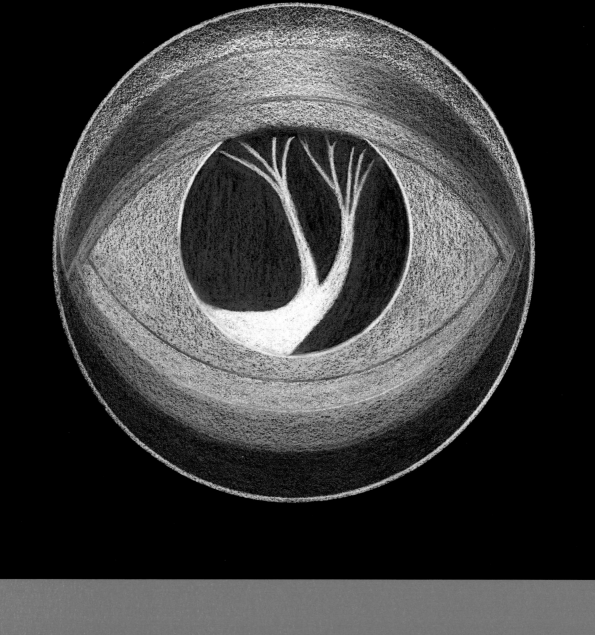

## *Pey* expresses the power of speech and the possibility of freedom.

Just as God creates the world through speech, we—as reflections of the Divine—also have the power to create. *Pey* instructs us to speak our thoughts consciously and with intention.

One story teaches that the world hangs in the balance between good and bad, love and fear, compassion and indifference. Whenever we speak we create an angel. When we speak in hurtful ways, we create negative angels. When we speak in gratitude, praise, and blessing, we create angels of goodness, love, and compassion. So *pey* speaks of choice. We have the freedom to create our world, and we are responsible for the world we create.

*Kavannah:*

**SPEAK KINDLY, WISELY, AND LOVINGLY. ENGAGE YOUR POWER AS A CO-CREATOR WHO MANIFESTS BLESSING AND HOLINESS IN THE WORLD.**

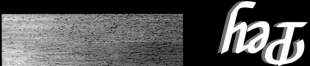
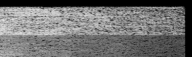

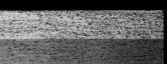

# *Tzadi*

## *Tzadi* commands us to open our hearts in service to others.

By performing acts of righteousness (*tzedakah*) and lovingkindness (*gemilut chasadim*), we connect with the Divine. Surrendering the ego is essential. When we act in humility, we are supported on a wave of Divine love. When we approach life with a commitment to being of service and acting in the highest good, the universe reflects back to us all that is good and abundant in the world.

*Kavannah:*

**WHAT GIFTS DO YOU GIVE TO THE WORLD WITH NO EXPECTATION OF RECOGNITION OR REWARD? WHAT GIFTS DO YOU RECEIVE UNBIDDEN?**

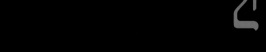

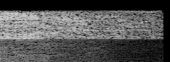

# *Koof*

### *Koof* **reminds us to become holy (***kadosh***).**

Growth is cyclical, with phases of activity and phases of rest. Through all cycles of our lives, we aspire to grow in connection with the Divine.

*Koof* directs us to the spiritual nature of our lives. The shape of the letter provides a clue: The top element represents the attainment of holiness (*kedusha*), and the bottom element is our dynamic yearning for spiritual union. As we grow in spirit, we create a space in which God may abide—and the *Shekhina*, sensing our movement toward connection, integration, and wholeness, enters and grows within us.

*Kavannah:*

**RECOGNIZE THE CYCLICAL NATURE OF GROWTH AND THE NEED FOR BALANCE. ALLOW AND ENCOURAGE YOUR SPIRITUAL GROWTH TO DEVELOP NATURALLY.**

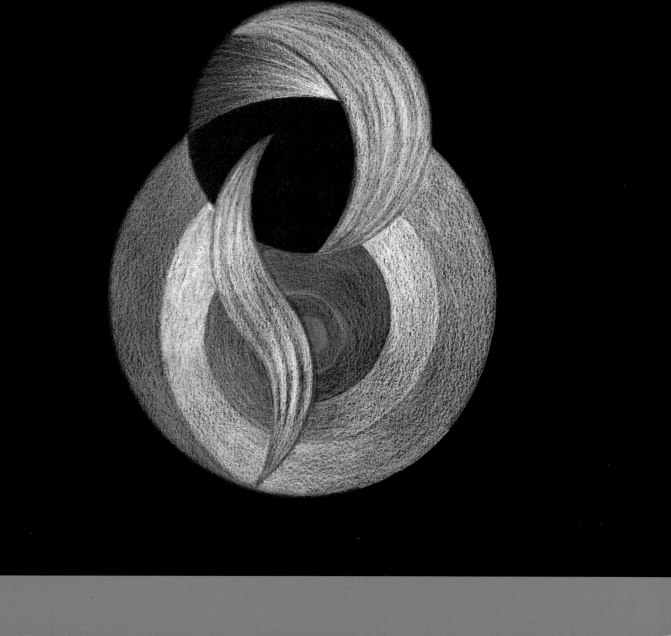

# Resh

**Resh reminds us that Divine essence is contained within us and within everything.**

*Resh* is the symbol for the mind (*rosh* = head). It is the mind that creates the cosmos in partnership with the Divine. Our perceptions shape reality. Every thought, every word, every action affords us a multitude of possibilities and opportunities for inner movement toward the Divine. We give our world meaning with our interpretations; we always have a choice in how we perceive our world. And with choice comes responsibility. So *resh* obligates us to interpret our reality in ways that honor the inherently Divine essence of everything.

*Kavannah:*

OBSERVE THAT YOUR REALITY IS SHAPED BY YOUR PERCEPTIONS. LISTEN TO OTHERS WHOSE PERCEPTIONS MAY BE DIFFERENT FROM YOURS. BE MINDFUL THAT WE CREATE OUR WORLD TOGETHER, THROUGH OUR SHARED REALITIES.

# *Shin*

***Shin* depicts the eternal fire that nourishes, purifies, and renews.**

Divine essence is like a flame. It is the cosmic fire that never dies. It feeds the spirit and nourishes the soul.

*Shin* is associated with fire (*aysh*) and the sun (*shemesh*). All Jewish celebrations begin with fire—a lighting of the candles. *Shin* is the fire that welcomes *Shekhina* and the peace (*shalom*) of the Sabbath (*Shabbat*).

*Kavannah:*

## VISUALIZE YOURSELF GLOWING WITH WARMTH AT THE CENTER OF YOUR BEING AND SURROUNDED BY LIGHT.

   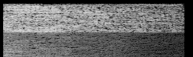

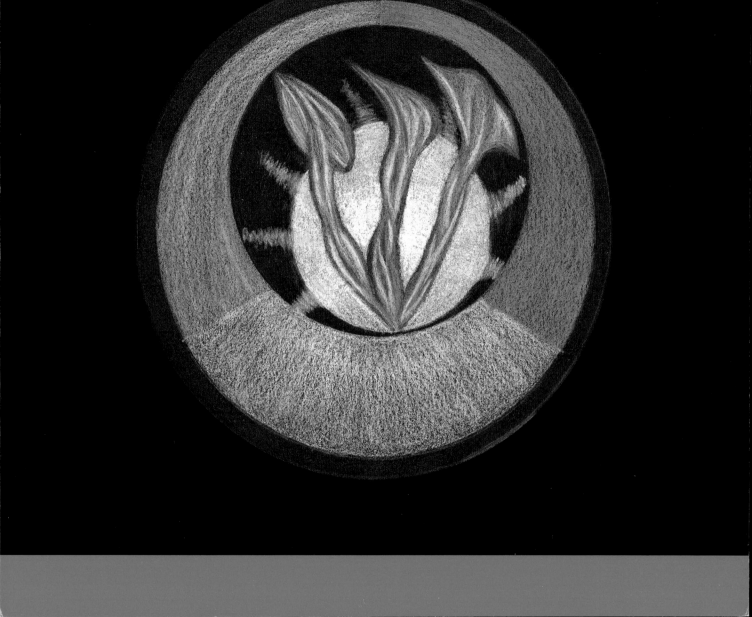

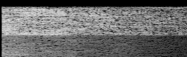

# Tav

**_Tav_ is the last letter—the final sound that precedes the return (_teshuvah_) to the oneness and silence of _aleph_.**

_Tav_ is the structure of Torah, grounding us in the physical world while allowing us to soar in the realms of holiness. As above, so below: What we do in this world reflects the spiritual world. Our thoughts, words, and actions connect us to God. When we live in accordance with Torah, we become bearers of holiness.

_Tav_ also is the sound of _tefillah_ (prayer) and _tehilim_ (praise) vibrating throughout the universe. The final sound of _emet_ (truth) is _tav_.

_Kavannah:_

**THERE ARE MANY PATHS TO TRUTH.
GO WITHIN AND FIND YOUR OWN, AND LIVE IT.**

# Suggested Reading

Cooper, David. 1997. *God is a Verb: Kabbalah and the Practice of Mystical Judaism*. New York: Riverhead Books.

———. 1995. *Renewing Your Soul: A Guided Retreat for the Sabbath and Other Days of Rest*. San Francisco, CA: Harper San Francisco.

Cornell, Judith. 1994. *Mandala: Luminous Symbols for Healing*. Wheaton, IL: Quest Books.

Ginsburgh, Yitzchak. 1990. *The Hebrew Letters: Channels of Creative Consciousness*. Jerusalem: Gal Enai Institute.

Glazerson, Matityahu. 1991. *Letters of Fire: Mystical Insights into the Hebrew Language* (translated by S. Fuchs). Jerusalem/New York: Feldheim Publishers.

Glotzer, Leonard R. 1992. *The Fundamentals of Jewish Mysticism: The Book of Creation and Its Commentaries*. Northvale, NJ: Jason Aronson.

Green, Arthur. 1999. *These Are the Words: A Vocabulary of Jewish Spiritual Life*. Woodstock, VT: Jewish Lights Publishing.

Haralick, Robert M. 1995. *The Inner Meaning of the Hebrew Letters*. Northvale, NJ: Jason Aronson.

Kaplan, Aryeh. 1985. *Jewish Meditation: A Practical Guide*. New York: Schocken Books.

———. 1995. *Meditation and Kabbalah*. Northvale, NJ: Jason Aronson.

———. 1997. *Sefer Yetzirah: The Book of Creation*. York Beach, ME: Samuel Weiser.

Kushner, Lawrence. 1990. *The Book of Letters: A Mystical Alef-Bait*. Woodstock, VT: Jewish Lights Publishing.

Munk, Michael L. 2001. *The Wisdom in the Hebrew Alphabet*. Brooklyn, NY: Artscroll Mesorah.

Prager, Marcia. 1998. *The Path of Blessing: Experiencing the Energy and Abundance of the Divine*. New York: Three Rivers Press.